LOVE YOURSELF

THE 30 DAY CHALLENGE TO

"SELF LOVE"

LOVE YOURSELF LIKE YOUR LIFE DEPENDS ON IT

BY: 30-DAY CHALLENGES

TABLE OF CONTENTS

INTRODUCTION

Have you disliked yourself for the majority of your life? Are you in complete and total unconditional love with yourself, presently? Are you able to honestly admit that you truly love yourself? If you have answered "no" to the last question, don't worry. There is still hope for you.

Self-love is not just an idea or concept that we create in our heads. Many of us have the crazy idea that if we are not taking care of everyone around us or working hard that we are being lazy and selfish. By doing these things, we tend to forget our value of self-worth and self-love. If we don't take care of ourselves, no one else is going to. We need to love ourselves and value ourselves to be the best we can for others.

With this book, "Love Yourself," you will find a 30 day challenge that teaches you how to love and accept who you are.

This is much more than just a collection of practical and fun exercises you can begin doing right away. It is actually an easy-to-read and implement roadmap of how you can begin loving yourself unconditionally. It is both simple and revolutionary. While reading this book, some of the things you will learn and discover include:

- A process that will help you identify the things that you have essentially been "duped" into not liking about yourself.

- How to flip these dislikes and love what you didn't love in the past.

- How you can become your own biggest cheerleader and fan. To forgive yourself as well as others and how to love who you are today.

- How you can create and use a self-love mantra to keep you on the path to total self-love.

- And more.

When you apply the exercises and steps you find in this 30 day self-love book, you will be able to discover both your outer and inner beauty and see what is truly magnificent about you like you never have in the past. You will become passionate about things in your life and when you are in love with the person you are today, you will find that your life is better in many, many ways.

This book represents the peace you have been missing. It is a road-map to building a life of prosperity, abundance, success, self-respect, self-acceptance and most of all...love.

Read the book, use the steps, and take a huge leap toward a life of happiness today.

When you have completed this 30 day challenge, take some time to look back on where you began just 30 days in the past. Chances are you are going to be amazed about how far you have come.

CHAPTER 1: DAYS 1 TO 5

Day 1: Start a Journal

The best way to get the most out of this book is by having a way to reflect on your activities and be able to go back to the starting point to see how far you have come since day one of this challenge.

One of the biggest benefits of journaling for this 30-Day Challenge is going to be reinforcing your feelings, and causing your mind to recollect the events of your activities. For example, let's say that on day 3 you do your activity in the morning but you do your journaling in the evening. By evening time, you may forget your boost in feelings that you felt after completing the activity that morning so when you sit down in the evening to reflect on your day, your mind reminds you of those feelings and reinforces the positivity that you felt afterwards.

Throughout this challenge, each day you will already have a prompt of what to journal about but on the days that you need an idea, here are some prompts that can help you reflect on yourself:

- What is one thing I love about myself?

- What does unconditional love look like to me?

- What is one thing that I do not like about myself, and why?

- What is something you really want to hear from someone?

- What makes me happy?

- What are 2 moments in your life when you felt the happiest about yourself?

Day 1 Activity: Today's activity is simple, use your journal and write about why you feel as though you do not love yourself the way you deserve. Make a list if you need to, just be sure to put everything down that you do not like about yourself and things that you wish you could change.

Day 2: Mirror, Mirror On the Wall...

For this exercise you need to look at yourself in the mirror – really look at yourself. Say the following: "I Love You," to your own reflection.

While you may feel a bit silly doing this for the first time, and it may seem somewhat pointless, you should still give it a try. While you may not think it will have very much of an impact on you, or how you feel, you are likely going to be pleasantly surprised.

For some people, it is actually difficult to utter the words – even when you do say them, your mind may be mocking you – "Yeah, right – that's a total lie. You don't love yourself."

The reason that quite a few people have issues with this exercise is because you have been taught to look into the mirror and point out everything you perceive to be a flaw.

You have to understand that you don't need someone else to validate your beauty. All you really have to do is see it and believe it. Far too many times you look to others to tell you that you are worthy, pretty and loveable, when you should be bestowing love on yourself.

Also, when you take the time to verbally acknowledge you don't like something about you, you are actually directing negative energy at that part of you and you may begin to see real problems.

When you are finally able to say "I Love You," to yourself and believe it, you will gain three amazing things:

1. You will no longer care about other's opinions of you.

2. Your self-esteem will increase significantly.

3. You will become so happy, attractive and confident that others are attracted to you effortlessly.

Day 2 Activity: When you look in the mirror, go further than just saying "I Love You." Point out a great feature and say why you love it – for example, I love you (your name) because (reason). Do this each morning for the entirety of the 30-day challenge, and don't forget to jot your feelings down in your journal.

Day 3: Shower Love Upon Yourself

This is an exercise that is fun, easy and something you can do without much effort every single day.

The first step is to get into the shower. While there, imagine that instead of water falling all over your body, that it is love you are being showered with. Try to point your finger at your shower head and state, "you are pouring love down on me." Imagine the water as pure love. If possible, visualize this and feel the "love" embedded in each drop that touches you.

As you wash your hair, tell it you love it – the way it feels, looks, smells – do the same with your body. Again, this may be something you feel a bit silly doing at first, but it really does put you in the mindset of loving yourself unconditionally.

The second step of this challenge is to dry off and apply lotion to your skin. Afterwards, do the Mirror exercise from day one again. Continue telling yourself how much you love and appreciate you.

When you consistently participate in the exercises from day one and day two, you will find that you are subtly shifting your vibration into a happier, more positive vibe.

Day 3: Activity: During your shower, imagine it is Love, not water, pouring all over you. While this may feel uncomfortable or sound ridiculous, it is a way to begin to feel that love that you have been missing. Write down your honest thoughts on this in your journal and describe how you felt afterwards.

Day 4: Get Specific: How Do You Love Yourself?

This is where the 30-day challenge becomes more exciting. Today, you are going to begin listing all the positive qualities about yourself. Everything you love about who you are needs to be put into your journal. For some, this can be quite challenging. Especially for those who have experienced abuse and criticism throughout their life. However, as you participate in these exercises you will find that loving yourself and finding reasons to love yourself becomes easier.

Today, your job is, in addition to the shower and mirror exercise, to think about all of your good qualities and then take some time to appreciate and bless them.

What do you really love about yourself? Take some time to make two different lists. One is where you will express appreciation and love for physical qualities and the other will be for your inner qualities. When you take the time to express love for a single aspect of yourself, you will be blessing that single aspect.

Make sure that you acquire 10 things on each of your lists. For internal beauty, think about your inner qualities, such as talents, skills and creativity.

You can use the formulas here to create your lists:

- I appreciate, love and bless my (physical trait) because (reason).

- I appreciate, love and bless my (skill or inner quality) because (reason).

While this may be difficult for some, it is important to keep going and get 10 things for each list. This is mainly because modern society has taught you to downplay your qualities and be modest. However, in making these lists, you are working to re-train your mind to embrace everything good that you have been ignoring for so, so long.

Day 4 Activity: Make two lists – one for physical and one for inner things you love about yourself in your journal. Review and add to these things regularly.

Day 5: Forgive Yourself

It can be difficult to learn to love yourself, especially if you have gone through the majority of your life hating various aspects.

One of the first things you must remember is that you are worth of love, from others as well as yourself. The goal of the program is to help you see yourself as perfect just the way you are and to love yourself unconditionally. This is not about how you look or how other perceives you.

Also, keep in mind, this is not a challenge that is asking you to delve into and face past traumas or experiences that may be hurting your ability to love yourself. However, in order to be rid of the pain and suffering you have felt in the past, you have to be willing to let go of it. The past is over and what you have now is the present, which is what creates your future. You have to learn to accept that.

The only way that you can successfully release yourself from all suffering and pain is with forgiveness.

This is difficult with a society that constantly calls out people's imperfections and issues, but something that should be done, none the less. In order to forgive yourself, use these steps.

- Identify everything you dislike about yourself and write these things down.

- Realize that these are things that are not "bad" or "good" but that they just are.

- Take each item that has been written down and say: "I forgive myself, and I forgive you" until you feel the negativity diminish.

- Give yourself the permission to let go.

Forgiving yourself is difficult, forgiving the hurt and pain that have made it difficult to love yourself is also difficult, but with time, you will find the negativity around how you look and feel is diminished and, eventually eliminated altogether.

Day 5 Activity: Today, you will learn to forgive yourself. Use the steps above to go through each thing you dislike about yourself and write them down in your journal.

Chapter 2: Days 6 to 10

Day 6: Find Ways To Be Good To Yourself

Today is considered a fun day in this 30-day challenge. The purpose of the exercise today is to find areas of your life where you are not good to yourself and then correct them. For example, do you stay up too late, or eat foods that aren't necessarily good for you?

Do you not eat enough or deprive yourself in some other way? Do you over-exercise, or under-exercise? Do you force yourself to participate in activities you don't really want to do? Are you mean to yourself? Do you overly criticize yourself and your actions? Is there something you have been wanting to do, but feel as though you don't deserve it?

You may wonder why it is so important to treat yourself kindly and be good to yourself. The fact is, when you aren't being good to yourself, you are sending a signal into the universe that essentially states that you are not important enough or worthy of good things. This means that the universe is going to be withholding certain things from you because you don't view yourself as important.

When you make the decision to be good to yourself, the Universe is going to follow and also be good to you. This is your motivation to treat yourself better.

Day 6 Activity: Simply do something good for yourself. Do something that is going to make you feel good about yourself that you normally don't do. Get your nails done, buy a new outfit, or simply take the day to turn your phone off and curl up with a good book. Whatever you choose to do, make it something that makes you feel good and something that you normally would not do. Write about your feelings afterwards in your journal. Describe how you felt when you were finished, if you feel better about yourself, emotionally or physically.

Day 7: Make Yourself a Priority

For many people, the ability to put themselves first is a difficult one. Many people say that this is something that is harder for women than it is for men. Women are mothers and therefore naturally want to take care of people around them, putting their own needs last.

This may be in spending money on yourself, or even taking time for yourself. Think about the kind of signal this is sending to the Universe – a signal that you are unworthy of good things.

When you fail to put yourself first, the Universe will also fail to put you first. By putting yourself first, your friends and family will see that you matter also, and will begin to do little things to put you first as well.

Today, you need to carefully consider how you can send the Universe the signal that you are a priority. Some ways you can do this include:

- Serve yourself first at dinner, and then others.

- Put your order in first when at a restaurant with friends and family.

- Be first when walking into or out of a building.

- When shopping, select something for yourself first and then choose for others.

Remembering that you are important too is a big part of loving yourself. Also, it is not necessary to spend money or to purchase something outrageous to show the universe that you are important, too.

Day 7 Activity: Put yourself before others. Let the universe know that you are important too. When you are writing in your journal about this activity, make sure to note your feelings. Did you feel guilty, liberated, important?

Day 8: Make Yourself the Star Of Your Own Movie

Today, you are going to be a movie star in the movie of your very own life.

Take some time to revisit the accomplishments you have made throughout your life and put them in your journal. Allow yourself the time to feel all the great emotions that you felt at the time of the accomplishment.

It is easy and likely second nature to think about all the mistakes you have made. This can cause you to begin second-guessing yourself and the decisions you make. However, when you focus on the good, amazing accomplishments you have made, you will find that your way of thinking alters.

With this exercise, you will begin to rebuild your self-respect and confidence. Rather than thinking about everything you have done wrong, you will think about all the different times that you did something right.

To begin this exercise, you will need to think about all the times you really rocked, when you won or did something great or extraordinary. Times when you were the center of attention, will also work. This can be a test you passed in school or a spelling bee that you won. It can also be job interviews that went really well, or when your husband proposed to you.

Be sure to write down all these amazing memories and each time you feel that feeling of "no love" review them and relive them.

These are the memories that can become the fuel for your happiness and help you out when you need a bit more job in your life.

It may be a good idea to read or relive these moments right before bed each night. Chances are you will sleep better and feel great in the morning.

Day 8 Activity: Write down memories when you really "rocked" something and the amazing way you felt. Add to these as you remember more memories, by unlocking these memories, you will begin to remember things that happened long ago that you may have forgotten about.

Day 9: Love Who You Are Right Now

For day nine, you looked at the past – your accomplishments and happy memories. Today, you get to celebrate the person you have become and give yourself and enormous pat on the back for the stellar job you are doing at just being yourself.

It can be difficult to be satisfied with the person you are today. This can be difficult because society teaches you to always look to the future and work to improve and to accumulate more material things. Only then are you allowed to be happy. As a result, not having these things or not having reached this destination can leave you feeling as though you are not good enough.

To participate in this exercise you need to take some time to smell the roses. Evaluate where you are in life today and who you are. What is it that you do? Create a list of all the little things that come to mind – mother, wife, writer, chocolate lover, etc. You can write anything that defines the person you are right now.

The next step is to accept that where and who you are right this very second is fine. In fact, it is perfect.

Take some time to really appreciate who you are and what you have accomplished in your life. Don't worry about tomorrow and don't think about yesterday. Take some time to appreciate and revel in who you are right this very second – after all, it is pretty amazing.

Day 9 Activity: Write as much as you can in your journal about who you are today and why you love who and where you are in life.

Day 10: Look To Your Bright Future

What is it that you want to achieve in life? What type of person would you like to be?

While you are perfect right now, you have to be honest – you would likely improve certain parts of yourself if possible.

Today, you are going to identify the areas in your life you would change or improve. Write down in your journal everything you want for your life – this can be wealth, laughter, humor, abundance and anything else that you desire.

This can be considered the brainstorming portion of your road-map to your future. To get what you want out of life, you have to have a starting point. This is it. By writing down exactly what you want, you now have the starting point of your journey.

Day 10 Activity: Write down where you would like to be in the future and what you can change now to achieve this goal. You can also elaborate and add as much detail as you would like on how you are going to reach those goals and steps you need to take to get there. Make sure to add you fears, doubts and concerns and come up with ways to turns those into something positive.

CHAPTER 3: DAYS 11-15

Day 11: Pay It Forward

It has been proven that by doing random acts of kindness for others who are less fortunate to you, can greatly improve your state of mind and your feelings of self-worth. By taking a little of our own time out of your day to do something that benefits someone else can leave you feeling very good about yourself.

For instance, the next time you are in the grocery store and the person in front of you is short on some change, give it to them, if you have it to spare. Or help someone who is struggling to get their groceries into their car. Little acts of kindness go a long way and are greatly appreciated by those on the receiving end of them.

Of course, there are larger acts of "Paying it forward" such as buying someone's meal, or taking on a task that is going to be very time consuming, but it is completely up to you on what you choose to do. No matter what you do, it is sure to be appreciated.

Paying it forward, is also a great way to help you get out and meet new people and to step out of your comfort zone if you are the type of person who normally feels isolated or isn't comfortable approaching new people. Just by saying "Here, let me help you" is a great icebreaker and can lead to a long lasting acquaintance or relationship if given the opportunity.

Here is a list of some examples that you can do to pay it forward:

- Shovel an elderly neighbor's sidewalk after it snows.

- Pay the toll of a driver that is behind you in line.

- Bake something for a neighbor.

- Offer to do an errand for someone that can't get out very often.

- Mow the neighbors grass when they are out of town.

- Pump gas for someone who is elderly when the weather is bad.

Day 11 Activity: Make it a point to do one random act of kindness for someone by paying it forward. When you are done, take a moment and write down your reflections on it. How did you feel? Were they appreciative? Were you uncomfortable approaching them to offer assistance?

You will find that by doing things like this more often, you will become more comfortable, and it will become second nature to want to help someone out, and make you love yourself even more in the process.

Day 12: Declutter Your Surroundings

How many times have you looked around at your home and thought, "I really need to go through this mess"? Only to find that you are completely overwhelmed and finally decide that the only that sees it is you. Scientific studies have shown that people who are not 100% happy with themselves, or have a feeling of low self-worth tend to have cluttered cars and homes.

Let's admit it, we all that that closet that we feel like we are going to get lost in if we try to find a shirt we haven't worn in a while, or that junk drawer that we pray a guest will not decide to open. Or the dreaded medicine cabinet that seems to be a magnet for guests that need to use the restroom. When we get caught up in how busy our lives are and how hectic our schedules become, we tend to let those things go and think "someday, I'll do that".

By decluttering your surroundings and bringing organization to your life, you will feel better about yourself because you will know that it is something you accomplished on your own. It is also a way of doing a good deed, if you are going to donate items to a charity or organization for those who are less fortunate.

Day 12 Activity: Choose one place in your home, or even your vehicle, and declutter it. Pick one drawer, one closet, one cupboard, or the trunk of your car and get rid of the items that you do not use or are no longer needed. If you are choosing a closet, donate your old clothing to a Goodwill or Salvation Army store.

Day 13: Recruit Help

Today is the day when you are going to let others in on your challenge. As hard as it may be to tell others what you are doing, it can be the most beneficial to you. Our friends and family can be our toughest and most honest critics. And while they love you, they may be able to shed some light on things that you can do to improve yourself and your view of yourself.

Day 13 Activity: For this activity, you are going to have to have some tough skin. Recruit your closest friends and family members. You can do this over the phone or in person. Tell them how you feel about yourself and the challenge you are doing. Ask them to give their opinions on things that you may be able to change about yourself that could make you feel better about yourself. Be prepared, they may notice things about you that you never realized and some of the things may not be wonderful and complimentary. Just remember, they love you unconditionally and would never intentionally do anything to hurt you. They are trying to help you and you are asking for their thoughts. Your journal entry for this activity may be pretty lengthy, but the more information you can gain, the more you have to make you a better person and love yourself even more as improvements are made.

Day 14: Find A New Hobby

Yesterday's activity was probably an emotional one, so today we are going to do something easy. Find a new hobby. While we all have things that we like to do in our spare time, those tend to get tedious and boring. Today you are going to find something new that you can take up as a hobby that you enjoy.

When we do things for ourselves that make us happy and are purely for pleasure, we feel a higher value of self-love because at the completion of our hobby project, there is a feeling of satisfaction and we are proud of what we have completed.

Take a moment to think about what you would like to do in your spare time. Are you interested in home DIY but have never attempted it? Do you find scrapbooking or photography interesting? Of course, everyone is different and enjoys different activities. And your personality plays a major role in what types of hobbies you'll enjoy.

Think about some of the things you already enjoy and how you could possibly expand on them. It may take a few different attempts before you find the right fit, but it can be a fun and exciting experience trying out new things and seeing what is out there.

Day 14 Activity: Try something new as a hobby. It doesn't have to be something that you have to stick with, just give something new a try. You may find that even if it wasn't something that you absolutely loved in the beginning, at the completion of it, you might have found something that you are incredibly good at and makes you love yourself even more. Make sure to keep a list of hobbies you try and explain the project you did and how you felt when you were completed.

Day 15: Reconnect With Old Friends

With social media and how hectic people's live have become, it is hard to remember to connect personally with people from your past. Reach out to your old group of friends from high school or college. Looking back, those times may have been the happiest in your life; when you felt invincible and great about yourself.

Too often we consider "staying in touch" to mean hitting the "like" button on someone's Facebook page. That isn't really staying connected. How many friends do you have on Facebook that you used to be close to but over time have lost touch with? Now is the time to reach out to them. Send them a message about meeting for lunch, or going to a concert if there is a group playing that is someone you used to listen to when you were younger.

Reconnecting with people from your past can help provoke positive memories of happy times when life was carefree, and you loved yourself, more than anyone else. Don't be afraid to get some of that self-love back. That is your goal, after all.

Day 15 Activity: Reach out to old friends. Reminisce about happy times and things you did together. By getting reacquainted with them, you can see where you started and how far you have come in life. Make sure to document in your journal about the experiences from your past, the fun times you had, as well as how you felt after meeting up with them. Are you proud of your achievements? Did you remember how you felt about yourself all those years ago when life was easy and fun? Write down anything that is positive.

CHAPTER 4: DAYS 16-20

Day 16: Self-Reflection

Congratulations! You have made it to the half-way point in your 30-day challenge! Today is all about looking back over the past two weeks and revisiting your journal entries to see how much improvement you have made.

While at first, you may not feel as though you have made much progress, when you read over your journal, you may start to see the way your wordings have changed. What may have started out as negative and not very complimentary of yourself may be slowly changing to a more positive outlook. In the beginning, you may have felt depressed, low self-esteem, and not worthy of certain things. Over the past two weeks, if you have been completing the activities, you have been pretty busy with new experiences, boosting your confidence and helping others.

Today is all about you! By looking over your journal, you will see a difference in how you feel about yourself and your general outlook on life. Think about different things that you can do if you were to repeat any of the activities over again.

Day 16 Activity: Relax and pull out your journal. Start at the beginning of your challenge from two weeks ago and read through all of your journal entries. As you do, reflect on how things have changed from the beginning. Jot down any additional items you want to add to the various lists you have made or make notes on how you feel that you have changed over the course of this challenge so far.

Day 17: Smile

Smiling is one of the easiest things that you can do to boost your feelings of self-love. When you smile, it activates the release of tiny molecules that send messages to your body that you are happy. Your smile makes you more approachable to others and opens up the door to meeting new people. It gives off a pleasant reaction and can benefit you in all aspects of your life. When you smile at others is shows a higher level of confidence and portrays the ability to handle difficult situations. This can be very beneficial in your career and leads people to view you in a favorable light.

Here are a few other benefits of smiling:

- It lowers stress and anxiety.

- It makes you more attractive.

- It is contagious. When you smile, others smile back.

- It can make you more comfortable in unfamiliar situations.

When you smile and give off a positive feeling, you invoke those positive feelings onto others and create an inner peace within yourself. When you notice that people are wanting to engage with you more because of your smile, you will begin to feel better about yourself and over time, your smile could become one of the things that you can add to your list about the things you love about yourself.

Day 17 Activity: Spend today smiling. When you pass a random stranger or are standing in the checkout line at a store, smile. If you are at work, and a coworker approaches you, instead of just looking at them and saying hello, smile while saying it. You will notice a change in how people respond. At the end of the day, when you are journaling about this, write down how you felt about yourself after seeing others reactions at your positive, pleasant attitude.

Day 18: Accept Compliments

When someone offers you a compliment, say "Thank you." Many times, we have a hard time accepting compliments. This is especially true for those of us who have a low level of confidence or feel that we aren't good enough. When people compliment you, it is because they genuinely feel that way about you. They really do like the outfit you have on or the new hairstyle you have. They aren't just saying it to make conversation.

When your boss tells you "Good work!" smile, say "thank you", and accept it. You deserve the compliments and should accept them without doubting their true meanings.

The same goes for when your significant other gives you a compliment. If he/she says "That shirt looks good on you", or "hey, you did a really good job on that" don't make excuses or debate what they say. Simply say "thank you" and accept the good feelings you get from it.

Day 18 Activity: Graciously accept compliments today. Throughout your day today, whenever someone gives you a compliment, accept it. Don't let that feeling of doubt take over. Remember that you are worthy of the compliments. In your journal keep track of the compliments you receive today and write down how you felt when you received them.

Day 19: Meditate

Meditation is a way of focusing your attention on one certain aspect to help you gain a clear awareness and understanding about your life. There are many health benefits to meditation such as:

- It decreases anxiety.

- Helps improve your emotional stability

- Increases your creativity

- Your happiness elevates

- Your intuition evolves

- You can gain peace of mind and clarity

- Your problems tend to seem smaller

- Increases your focus

By spending a few minutes every day meditating, it can help improve your mood and your outlook on life because it gives you inner peace. Problems don't seem to appear as bad as what you thought when you take the time to meditate.

When you meditate, be sure to focus on yourself and your positive qualities. By concentrating on the good qualities that you possess, you reinforce in your mind why you are worthy and what there is to love about you.

Day 19 Activity: Spend 10 minutes meditating. Take the time for yourself to focus on your own wellbeing and to reflect on your good qualities that make you the wonderful person you are.

Day 20: Put Extra Effort Into Your Appearance

So this one is pretty much a no-brainer! We all know that we feel better when we look good. Ladies, we all know that when we put the extra effort into our appearance that we generally feel good about ourselves. We have all had those moments when we need to make a quick run to the grocery store in our sweatshirt and yoga pants with our hair pulled back into a ponytail, and we tend to run into everyone we know. And then afterward we have that feeling of "I wonder what they think of me", and are somewhat ashamed of ourselves for going out like that. It's not just the ladies that do that; men do it also. Instead of taking those few extra minutes to prepare ourselves for the public, we allow that inner voice take over and say "oh well, it's not like I'm a supermodel anyway."

When we put the extra effort into our appearance and "dress to impress" we feel good about ourselves because we know we look good. It boosts our confidence when facing the outside world and gives us a feeling of "I'm worth it".

Day 20 Activity: When getting ready for your day, take the extra few minutes to put on makeup, do your hair, or wear that nice outfit that has been hanging in your closet. Throughout the day notice how differently people approach you and how you feel better about yourself overall.

Chapter 5: Days 21-25

Day 21: Let Go Of Your Comparisons To Other People

We all have those feelings of wanting to be like someone else, or wishing we had something that someone else has. By spending our life wishing and comparing ourselves to other people, we forget about the good things that we possess that others might wish they had. Maybe someone wishes they had your laugh or your easygoing personality. Comparing yourself to others only reinforces the feelings of unworthiness, and not being good enough.

When you are content with who you are inside, and stop comparing yourself to others, you realize that it doesn't matter what others possess that you do not. Your family and friends love you for who you are. You don't need to try to be like someone else to love yourself more. Love who you are, everyone else does!

Jealousy is an evil beast that can tear us to pieces if we let it. Feeling jealousy is not showing self-love, because it reflects unhappiness about what you don't have, instead of appreciation for what you do have. Be happy for others when good things happen to them. When you can be happy for someone else when they gain something, it makes you feel good inside and increases your level of self-love for yourself.

Day 21 Activity: Love who you are. Spend 15 minutes telling yourself that you love who you are and that you are glad that you are unique. Highlight the personality traits that you have that set you apart from everyone else. Think back to things that people have told you in the past that they love about you. It could be your witty personality, your attention to detail, your ability to really listen to other, or even something small like they way you laugh, or how dependable you are. Write these down in your journal.

Day 22: Try A Yoga Class

There are many benefits to taking a Yoga class, not only is it physically therapeutic, but it also serves as a huge benefit to your emotional and mental health. Every day your mind goes back and forth between the past and the future and in on a constant stream of thoughts, doubts, fears, worries, and overall negativity. By becoming aware of our thoughts, we care able to stop this cycle. Through Yoga, you are able to achieve a composed and a more mindful awareness

With Yoga, we learn to become more present in our own body, by making our subconscious to feel safe, allowing our bodies to relax. Many notice an emotional release after the end of the Yoga class and feel lighter, and less burdened. This can be a great way to release all of those negative feelings you may feel about yourself and try to connect with the positive attributes you have.

Day 22 Activity: Take a Yoga class. Many gyms offer your first few classes for free. Take advantage of that and give it a try. In your journal, at the end of the day, write down how you felt at that moment when the Yoga class was done. Did you feel positive and good about yourself?

Day 23: Practice Saying "No"

Sometimes learning to love yourself means having to tell others no. When you have a low self-esteem, you tend to overstretch yourself to make everyone happy. You will go out of your way to do favors for others because you do not want to tell them no and upset them.

It's okay to say "no" to people if it is something you really do not want to do. Many of us tend to feel as though if we do not say yes, that it will not get done or that we will come off as being rude or mean. Sometimes, it is just not possible for us to do what is asked and to say yes, just so that you won't upset anyone does nothing but cause more stress. When you are practicing self-love it is okay to say "no" or "no, I can't this time," to avoid adding that stress to ourselves.

It is not fair to yourself to take on more than you can handle just to make others like you more or to get that feeling of acceptance. When we love ourselves, we know that if we tell someone no that they will still love us and understand that we simply are not able to do it.

Day 23 Activity: Today, when someone approaches you with a task or favor that you do not want to do, say "no." Briefly, explain to them why you are unable to. If you are not ready to tell someone "no," practice at home. Run through mock conversations with yourself of someone asking you to do something and what your answers will be. With enough practice, you should be able to feel confident enough to tell someone no to something without the feeling of guilt or fear that they will be upset with you.

Day 24: Accept Yourself

Many of us that have a low self-esteem or who do not love our-selves know right off the bat that it is because we do not like our appearance. We may view ourselves as too fat, or too short. Our hair may not be the color or texture we want. A lot of it revolves around our physical appearance.

Once we begin to accept our appearance for the way it is, we will begin to see an improvement. You don't have to be 100% happy with your body to accept it and love it, just know that it is your body and feel comfortable in your own skin. By focusing on the negative parts of your body, you are overlooking all of the wonderful, positive qualities that you have.

To reach unconditional self-love means that you have to learn to love all of you, the good along with the bad.

Day 24 Activity: With your journal close by, stand in front of the mirror. Take a good look at yourself write down 10 things about your appearance that you do not like. Is there anything that you can do to change it? Why do you not like these things about you? Write down your feelings and for every negative answer, write down a positive answer.

Day 25: Hug Yourself

Yes, this may seem small and silly, but it works! Hugs can be very therapeutic, even on those instances when you receive them from yourself. Hugs touches and caresses all have lingering results and do more than just feel good at the moment.

How many times have you had a significant other or a close friend walk up and hug you for no reason? Do you remember how you seemed to have your burdens lifted, if only for a few minutes? Hugging has the same effects as smiling. It releases that "feel good" feeling and can lift someone's spirits.

Day 25 Activity: For one minute when no one is around, wrap your arms around yourself and give yourself a hug. You may feel funny doing this the first few times, but you will get used to it. Close your eyes and appreciate how good you feel, tell yourself "I love you" as you hug yourself. Write down your feelings in your journal.

CHAPTER 6: DAYS 26-30

Day 26: Value Yourself

If you don't value yourself, it is hard to love yourself. Hold yourself in high regard. If someone is seeking you out for your skills or knowledge that is of monetary value, charge what you are worth. Do not sell yourself short. If you know that you are good at what you do, don't be afraid to let others know that you are good also. By telling yourself that you are good, and having pride in yourself, others will too. Don't be afraid to congratulate yourself for a job well done.

Day 26 Activity: In your journal, write down the different ways you value yourself. Whether is it through a monetary value for the work you do, or by compliments that others give to you. When you place a high value on yourself, it shows a high level of confidence and leads to loving yourself even more.

Day 27: Count Your Blessings

You have probably heard this many times, but it is true. If you want to gain a higher level of self-love, focus on what you have and what you are blessed with. Make a list of all of the things that you are grateful for, that make you feel good; that brings a smile to your face.

Usually, the only time that we count our blessings is around Thanksgiving time, bit it is something that we should do on a regular basis so that we don't forget all that we have to be appreciative of.

The more that you learn to appreciate your blessings, the more you will begin to appreciate yourself, and that leads to you falling in love with yourself even more than you already do. Always look for things to be thankful for, it will make you realize how wonderful you really are.

Day 27 Activity: Make a list of 15 things that you are grateful for and blessed with. They can be small things or very important things that you hold in high regard. Make your list and as you write each one down, think to yourself why you consider this to be a blessing.

Day 28: Choose What Is Best For You

We all have those things that we think that we should do. Whether the request comes from someone else or if it is just something that we feel like we need to do for someone else, stop and think to yourself "Am I doing this for the right reason?"

Is it something that YOU want to do, whether it is for someone one else or not? If deep down you genuinely want to do it, and it is in your own best interest, this is telling you "I love you." By putting your own interests first and doing what is best for you shows that you hold yourself of high importance and are looking out for your own wellbeing.

We all have had those situations where we have done things that I felt obligated to do or the situations where we know that we can find a higher paying job, but stay where we are because we don't want to let anyone down. When these occasions arise, it is okay to tell yourself that you need to do what is best for you. By doing things to better yourself or make yourself feel good, you are showing that you are loving yourself and treat yourself as you would treat those around you that you love.

Day 28 Activity: Today do one thing that is in your best interest. Do something for yourself that you normally would do for someone that you love. When faced with a situation, stop and think "what's best for ME." In your journal, reflect on some things that you have missed out on because of putting yourself below others needs or wants. Think of how the outcomes could have been different if you had put yourself first.

Day 29: Let Go Of Your Inner Perfectionist

We all have that inner perfectionist inside of us that expects things to turn out a certain way. This causes us to become our own worst critic and to judge ourselves more harshly that others normally would. We cannot be perfect all of the time and need to learn to accept our flaws. Constantly striving for perfection can only reinforce a low self-esteem. There are always going to be flaws that we see in ourselves or areas that need improvement. By accepting these flaws and learning to love them, we can lose some of that low self-esteem and know what it truly means to love ourselves.

Why is it that when we think of our families and friends we think of their flaws and still love them unconditionally but we feel as though we can't love ourselves unconditionally with our flaws? If we can accept others flaws and love them regardless, we should be able to do the same for ourselves.

Day 29 Activity: Look in the mirror and tell yourself all of the flaws that you believe that you have. Write them down. Tell yourself that your flaws are what make you who you are and without them, you wouldn't be you.

Day 30: Love Yourself Unconditionally

This is the final day of the 30-day challenge. Today, just like day 15, is a recollection day of all that you have discovered about yourself on your journey to self-love. Your activity for today is to reflect over your entire journal and take notes on how you have progressed over the 30 days. Take notes on some things that you still want to change or work on. While 30 days is not a long period of time, every little bit of progress helps.

Write down in your journal 20 things that you now love about yourself. This should be easier than when you first began at the beginning of the challenge, as you have emotionally grown and learned to accept your flaws.

Conclusion

Congratulations! You have made it through your 30-day challenge to self-love. While at times some of the activities may have seemed silly or awkward, you stuck with them. Even some of the activities that caused you to dig a little deeper emotionally have helped in your progress over the last month, and they have worked.

I hope that now, at the end of your challenge, you feel a level of love for yourself that you did not have before you began. You need to remember each and every day that you are worthy of love, whether it is coming from yourself, or others. Throughout the course of this book, you were given activities to do every day to gain a better understanding of why you may have felt the way you did and what you could do to turn that around. The journey to self-love is usually an emotional one, but at the end of the journey, it is so worth it.

Keep journaling; it can only serve to help you in the future and give you a record of things that you desire to change and to see how you are progressing. The journey to self-love is a never ending one and can only deepen your love for yourself.

Thank you for taking the time to purchase this book and following the steps to learn how to love yourself. Always remember to take pride in yourself and keep telling yourself "I'm worth it!"

Made in the USA
Columbia, SC
11 September 2019